KU-242-185

21st-century SCIENCE

ELECTRONICS

Present knowledge • Future trends

Written by Moira Butterfield

W
FRANKLIN WATTS
LONDON•SYDNEY

This edition 2007

First published in 2004 by Franklin Watts

Copyright © Franklin Watts 2004

Franklin Watts
338 Euston Road
London NW1 3BH

Franklin Watts Australia
Level 17/207 Kent Street
Sydney NSW 2000

A CIP catalogue record for this book is
available from the British Library.

Dewey number 621.381

ISBN 978 0 7496 7383 3

Printed in China

Franklin Watts is a division of Hachette
Children's Books, an Hachette Livre
UK company.

Consultant Simon Maddison

Artwork Ian Thompson
Design Billin Design Solutions
Editor Constance Novis
Art Director Jonathan Hair
Editor-in-Chief John C. Miles
Picture Research Diana Morris

Picture credits

Dr Jeremy Burgess/SPL: 4-5 background, 32t
Tony Buxton/SPL: 26b
Corbis: 8b
Tony Craddock/SPL: front cover bc, 6, 12t
Malcolm Fielding, The BOC Group Plc/SPL: 24t
Simon Fraser/SPL: 27t
Lawrence Lawry/SPL: 30c
Dick Luria/SPL: 25b
Maximilian Stock Ltd/SPL: 9t
Astrid & Hanns-Frieder Michler/SPL:
front cover c, back cover background, 23t
Sam Ogden/SPL: front cover bl, 41b
David Parker/Seagate Microelectronics Ltd/SPL:
29b
Rosenfeld Images Ltd/SPL: front endpapers, 16t,
20b, 31t
Chris Sattlberger/SPL: front cover br, back
endpapers, 38c, 39b, 45
Dennis Scott/Corbis: 36b
Volker Steger/SPL: 40t
Andrew Syred/SPL: 33b
Tek Image/SPL: front cover t, 10b, 35r
Charles D. Winters/SPL: 28b

*Every attempt has been made to clear copyright.
Should there be any inadvertent omission, please
apply to the publisher for rectification.*

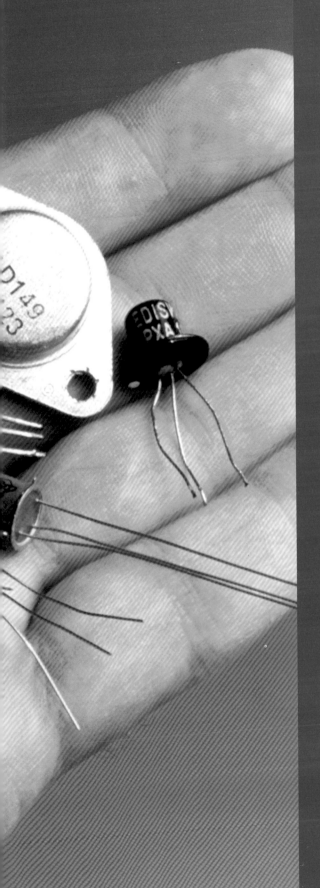

Contents

the world goes electronic

From the moment you wake up to the minute you go to sleep, your life is affected by electronics. Only a few decades ago this wouldn't have been true, but electronics has changed the world with incredible speed and is set to continue doing so in ever more powerful ways.

Your personal science

Some electronics are easy to spot. For instance, computers are electronically operated and there are more and more of them in the home, at school and at work. But if you think about your daily routine, you will discover just how much of it depends on hidden electronics. The alarm clock that wakes you up, the vehicle that takes you to school or work, the mobile phone you use to text a friend, the CD player, the washing machine, the microwave and the TV set – none of them would work without electronics inside them.

In with the new

Your TV, mobile phone and CD player are just a handful of examples that demonstrate how the science of electronics has improved life. It's everywhere. In fact, the technology is so pervasive but so often unseen that we have begun to take it for granted.

Yet only a couple of generations ago the machines people used in everyday life were mechanically operated, which meant they were much slower and less powerful than modern versions, and they took more work from humans to keep them going. Can you imagine having to wind up your music system by hand every time you want to hear a new release? If you lived 80 or 100 years ago that's exactly what you'd have to do.

All about electrons

At the heart of the science of electronics is the study of tiny particles called electrons. They are found inside atoms, the tiny building blocks that make up every kind of material in the world.

Each electron carries some electric charge. A stream of electrons can be made to move as an electric current through certain substances, and the behaviour of the current can be controlled in different ways.

The discovery and development of the idea that electrons can be used and controlled is the basis of all modern electronics.

Changing lives

The science of electronics has actually been around for more than 100 years. It evolved from work carried out in other fields of science such as electricity, electromagnetism and radio waves. Gradually it has developed, as more pieces have been added to the jigsaw of scientific knowledge.

The field of electronics is likely to continue changing fast. Although we now know the basic concepts, people are always thinking up new ways to use them, and new knowledge is constantly emerging.

Learn those basics and you, too, could join in the race to change the way we live.

▲

This photograph shows the inside of a factory for making electronic components in Bavaria, Germany.

◄ ◄

In 1900, gramophones (record players) such as this were wound up by hand.

CIRCUITS and SIGNALS

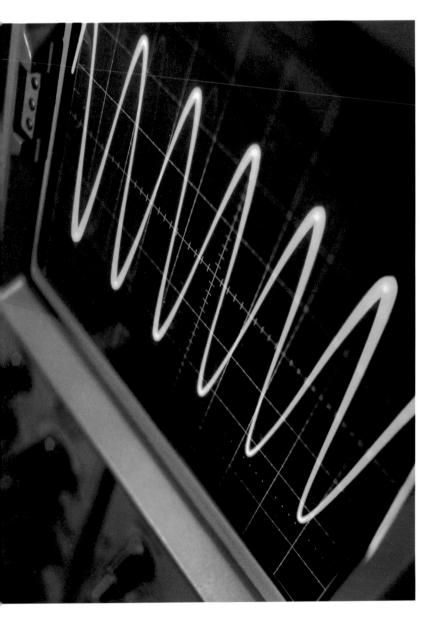

Electric current is a flow of electrons through a pathway called a circuit. The circuit is the basic tool of electronics. It carries signals in the form of an electric current.

The secret of circuits

A circuit requires a power source, such as a battery, and a pathway, such as a wire, through which the current can flow. There must be two terminals on the power source; one positively charged and one negatively charged.

Electrons carry negative electrical charge. They are repelled by the negative terminal and attracted to the positive one, and they flow around the circuit from one to the other. If the circuit is broken then the current will stop flowing.

In electronic equipment, circuit parts (called components) are put on a small flat circuit board or onto a tiny chip (see page 20).

Electric current

There are two sorts of electric current. Direct current moves at a steady rate in one direction unless it is switched off. Alternating current can vary, moving faster or slower, backwards or forwards.

Using a machine called an oscilloscope it's possible to measure electric current. On the oscilloscope screen an alternating current looks like a line of moving waves.

The height of each wave is called the amplitude, and the distance between wave peaks is called the wavelength. The number of waves in a given time is called the frequency. The pattern of the wave is the signal.

Analogue signals

There are two kinds of signal used in electronics. An analogue signal is one that comes from a current flowing along in an uninterrupted line of waves.

There are problems with analogue signals. They lose strength the further they travel, just like waves on water. They can also become distorted. You can hear this when the sound of an ordinary radio starts going fuzzy, perhaps if a vacuum cleaner gets switched on nearby. An ordinary radio signal is analogue and the cleaner's electric motor interferes with it.

Digital signals

In a digital device an analogue signal is sampled, or measured, at fixed intervals, and the measurements are converted into a string of numbers.

The string of numbers is then transmitted as a series of electrical pulses. At the other end, the pulses are read like a code and converted back into analogue waves by a decoder. They are recreated in as perfect a form as the initial signal.

A digital signal can be kept high quality however far the pulses travel, and it can be easily stored using electronic memory (see pages 18-19).

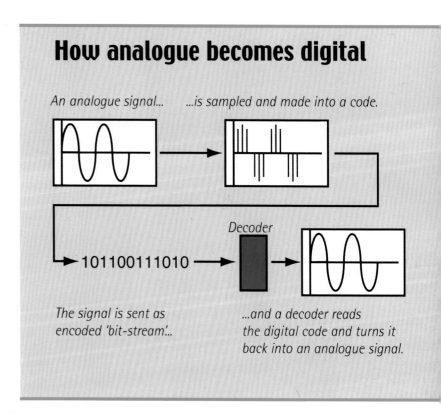

How analogue becomes digital

An analogue signal... *...is sampled and made into a code.*

101100111010

Decoder

The signal is sent as encoded 'bit-stream'...

...and a decoder reads the digital code and turns it back into an analogue signal.

▲

How an analogue signal is converted to a digital one.

◄ ◄

A machine called an oscilloscope displays an electric current as a wave pattern.

A fundamental discovery, the semiconductor, kick-started the revolution in electronic science when it was used to invent the transistor in the 1940s. The new device was first used in portable transistor radios in the 1950s and 1960s, so it helped kick-start pop music, too!

the BIG Discovery

A display of early transistors, used in radios during the 1950s and 60s.

This diagram shows how a transistor works.

Semiconductors

When the pioneers of electronics studied different materials they found that some had 'free electrons' that moved easily inside them. These they called 'conductors' because they could conduct an electric current. Other materials had no free electrons able to move. They were named 'insulators' because they could not conduct electricity. However, there is a third type of material, called a semiconductor, which will not normally conduct electricity, but can be made to do so if its electrons are given a little extra energy, boosting them enough to make them move.

Secrets of the crystal

The earliest radios were called 'crystal sets' because they used a crystal of a natural substance called galena to detect radio signals. Scientists knew that by moving a thin wire over the crystal they could find a 'sweet spot' where reception was particularly good, but they had no idea why. When they finally cracked the secret the science of electronics took a big leap forward.

The 'sweet spot' was in fact an impurity, a kind of fault line, inside the crystal. On one side the crystal had an area containing many free electrons, called the n-type area. On the other side there was a section with few or no free electrons, called the p-type area.

When the crystal picked up the radio signal it gave the free electrons in the n-type area enough energy to cross over to the p-type area, creating a current flow. The crystal was a semiconductor.

Science sandwich

Once scientists knew how the galena crystal worked, they went on to invent a device with a slice of p-type material between two pieces of n-type material.

A tiny current applied to the p-type material could create a big flow of electrons between the two n-type pieces, making the current much bigger than it was originally, or amplifying it.

The basis of a transistor is that it can quickly make a small current much bigger, and it can switch the current on and off as well.

Shrinking systems

The first use of the transistor was in small portable radios. The first ones had only one or two large transistors inside them.

Gradually transistors have been made smaller and smaller, and that's why modern music systems and computers look so much smaller than old versions, yet are much more powerful. They contain millions of tiny transistors on a few complex circuits.

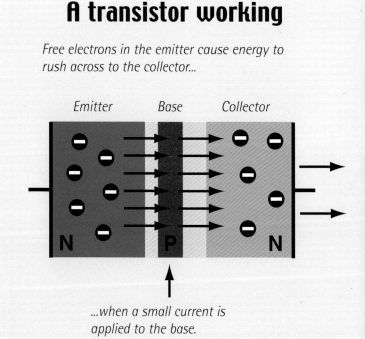

A transistor

Section called the emitter Section called the base Section called the collector

N   P   N

A transistor working

Free electrons in the emitter cause energy to rush across to the collector...

Emitter   Base   Collector

N   P   N

...when a small current is applied to the base.

inCONTROL

Electronics is all about controlling electric current to make it do something useful in a machine. To achieve this you must build a circuit using components, each one doing a different job to control the current.

Active components

A transistor is an 'active component', which means it does something to change the size of a current. It only needs a very small signal applied to it in order to produce a much bigger signal. This effect, amplification, is the basis of most electronic music systems. It's the reason, for instance, that a small signal from an electric guitar can be amplified loud enough to fill an entire stadium with sound.

As well as amplifying a signal a transistor can switch current on and off very quickly. In high-speed systems a transistor can switch on and off millions of times a second.

► ►

Electronic engineers use a set of specific symbols to identify components in circuit diagrams.

Passive components

Passive components do not amplify a current, but they can affect its flow and direction. Capacitors, resistors and diodes are all passive components. They each have a different function and their own symbol used in circuit drawings.

Capacitors

A capacitor is a component that stores an electric charge. It is made from two electrical plates with a gap between them. A capacitor will block direct current, but it will let alternating current through.

When connected to a power supply a capacitor fills up with charge. It can store it and then discharge it very quickly to power something.

An electronic camera flash is a good example of a capacitor discharging power quickly.

Resistors

A resistor is a component which reduces the flow of electrons through a circuit, to reduce the current strength.

Some resistors reduce current by a fixed amount. Some can be varied. For instance, when you twiddle the volume control on a radio, a variable resistor allows less or more current to travel through to the transistor which then amplifies it.

Diodes

Diodes are semiconductors (see page 12). They only let current pass one way, so they help to protect other circuit components from harm. For instance, a battery-powered device might contain a diode so that if you accidentally inserted the battery the wrong way round, the diode would block any current that might go in the wrong direction and damage the device.

Diodes come in many shapes and sizes. Some of them are LEDs, light-emitting diodes, which means they convert power into light. You'll find LEDs in electronic bicycle lights and torches.

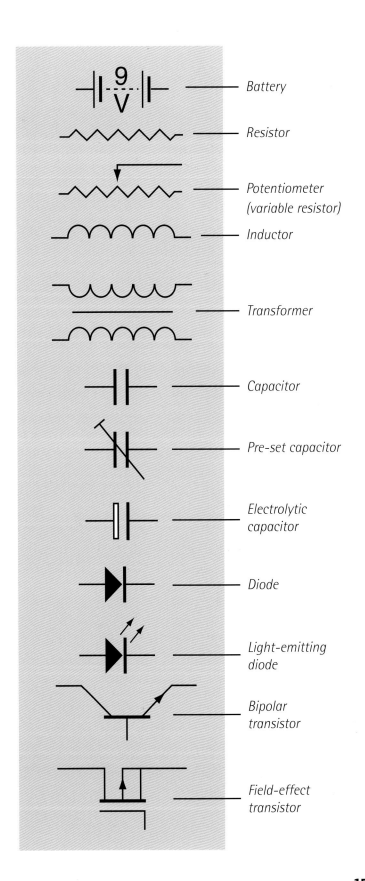

Battery

Resistor

Potentiometer (variable resistor)

Inductor

Transformer

Capacitor

Pre-set capacitor

Electrolytic capacitor

Diode

Light-emitting diode

Bipolar transistor

Field-effect transistor

Computer
BUILDING
BLOCKS

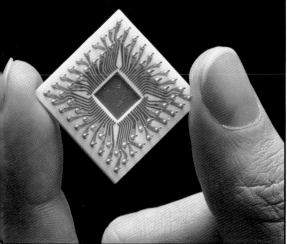

Electronic engineers have been able to construct different kinds of electronic building blocks using simple circuit components. The most important of these building blocks is the 'flip-flop'.

A modern integrated circuit contains millions of transistors.

Flip-flops

Two transistors can be connected in a circuit so that they control each other. When one switches on, the other switches off, and vice versa. The circuit can flip from one state to the other, which is why this arrangement is called a 'flip-flop'.

A flip-flop can be designed to stay in one configuration until an external trigger, such as a switch, makes it flip to the opposite configuration. This is called a 'stable flip-flop'.

A flip-flop sits in one state or the other, depending on whether it is on or off. This 'on or off' information is interpreted by a computer as binary digits, either 0s or 1s. These numbers are called bits.

A line of binary digits, called a 'bit-stream', is a code that the computer can read and store as data.

Flip-flops get together

A sequence of bits – 0s and 1s – can be stored by connecting a series of flip-flops together. This is called a 'shift register'.

An eight-bit shift register can store eight bits, which is usually called a

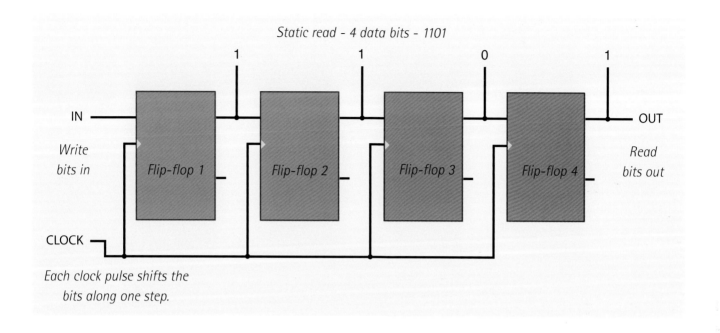

Static read - 4 data bits - 1101

1   1   0   1

IN

Write bits in

Flip-flop 1   *Flip-flop 2*   *Flip-flop 3*   *Flip-flop 4*

OUT

Read bits out

CLOCK

Each clock pulse shifts the bits along one step.

'byte'. A modern PC contains many megabytes (one megabyte equals a million bytes) of semi-conductor memory. That means an awful lot of flip-flops!

Millions of microscopic flip-flops etched on to tiny slices of silicon called chips (see page 24), along with other components, make what is called an 'integrated circuit'.

Sounds easy...

Lots of circuits can be put on one very small piece of silicon, but there are problems to be overcome. For instance, it might be necessary for lots of tiny signals to travel across the chip from different areas, yet arrive at the same point at the same time. An electronic designer needs to design the circuit components to make sure that happens. In very complex circuits that's a big challenge.

Cool your flip-flops

Complex integrated circuitry needs lots of power to operate properly, and that power produces heat.

In a small silicon chip the temperature can rise very high, but semiconductors only work in a limited temperature range – between 10° and 60° C. If things get too hot, a circuit won't work properly. That's the reason why there is a fan in a PC. Very powerful computers may even use liquid nitrogen to cool their chips.

▲

A line of flip-flops connected together is called a shift register.

Memory

Every electronic control system relies on memory to store its data.

This diagram demonstrates the difference between RAM and ROM in a modern computer.

What is data?

In an electronic piece of equipment some stored data will be the program instructions that control the system in the first place. Some might be data that is gathered during an operation – for instance words or numbers in a document written on a word processor. Spoken words, music and moving pictures can all be stored too.

However, all data of whatever kind, is always stored electronically as binary code – a series of 0s and 1s.

Making the code

A stream of binary digits might come from flip-flops switching on and off (semiconductor memory). It might come from the measurement of magnetic particles that are polarised to either north or south (called magnetic memory storage and used in hard disks in PCs). It might come from the measurement of a laser beam that reflects – or not – from a surface (optical memory storage, used for CDs and DVDs). But whichever method is used to read the signals 'on' or 'off', the information gets converted into a binary bit-stream in the end.

Non-volatile memory

To do its job, a piece of electronic equipment must contain some data that is permanently stored inside it, data that does not disappear forever when the machine gets switched off. Some of this 'non-volatile' memory is called ROM (read-only memory). ROM stores data such as the original program the designer built into the equipment in the first place; it cannot be changed.

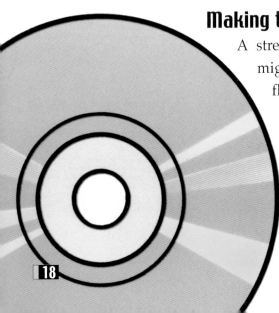

In a PC, working data is usually saved into magnetic memory. This means it is stored in a pattern of rings called tracks marked on a spinning hard disk. A tiny head hovers over the tracks, reading a series of magnetic signals representing 'on' and 'off'. These signals get converted into bit-streams of binary code for other parts of the machine to work with.

RAM

When an electronic machine starts working, the data that it needs to start operating is read from the ROM. Other working data is then moved from the relatively slow magnetic memory of the hard disk to a much faster memory called RAM (random-access memory). In RAM data is stored with a set of coordinates, as if it were on a map. This makes it much quicker to retrieve than the hard disk method of a head moving over tracks.

RAM is temporary or 'volatile' memory. When a machine gets switched off the data in the RAM disappears. The words on this page are temporarily held in RAM as they are written on a PC. But the author must save them before switching off, or they will be lost. When saved they are put in non-volatile memory such as the hard disk.

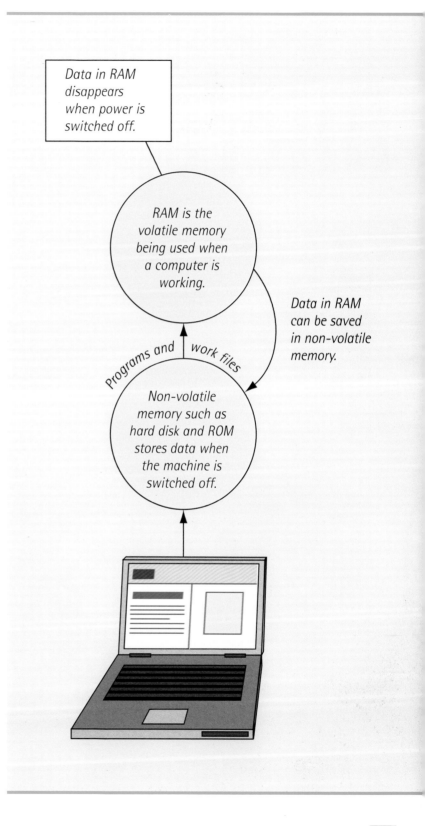

Data in RAM disappears when power is switched off.

RAM is the volatile memory being used when a computer is working.

Data in RAM can be saved in non-volatile memory.

Programs and work files

Non-volatile memory such as hard disk and ROM stores data when the machine is switched off.

At the heart of every active electronic system there is a microprocessor, a chip that can do lots of different jobs. The microprocessor was first introduced in 1971 by the company Intel.

Microprocessors

Brains of the business

A microprocessor is the brain of an electronic system. It makes everything happen. It can receive data, store it, read it and act on it. The hard-working heart of a microprocessor is called a CPU (Central Processing Unit).

A microprocessor connects to ROM and RAM and has some memory of its own to help it do its tasks. It also has input, so it can receive data from, say, a keyboard, and it has output, so it can send data to, for instance, a display or a printer.

A microprocessor uses logic calculations to translate digital program instructions into orders (see page 22). It sends on the orders to make the system work in a particular way. It can also move data from one memory to another and it can make decisions, for instance to jump to a new set of instructions.

Its components include a counter that helps it work methodically through a stream of step-by-step instructions. It contains registers that hold the data it receives, and it contains an 'arithmetic logic unit' that does sums to translate received data into orders.

Usually a small microprocessor chip is embedded inside a protective shell with pins around it to connect it to other circuits in the system. Connected to the pins are 'buses', bundles of wires that carry binary signals to and from other parts of the computer.

Small microprocessors

Small simple microprocessors are used in lots of familiar products. Sometimes called 'micro-controllers', they are embedded within a machine to make it work. For instance, a washing machine, a central heating timer or a pocket calculator might contain a micro-controller.

Once a program is written for one of these popular mass-produced products it can be permanently attached to a standard cheap-to-produce microprocessor in a piece of memory. This is called 'mask programming'. The same type of microprocessor might be used in lots of different products, with different masked programs attached to make the microprocessor work in different ways.

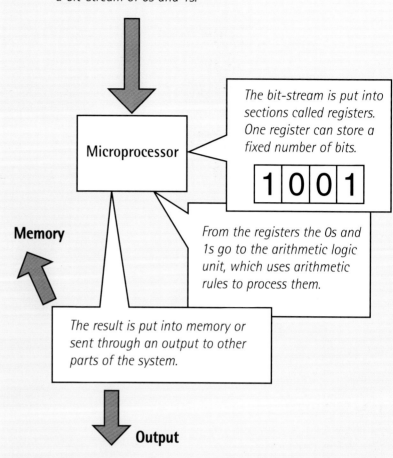

A microprocessor receives instructions from a program as a bit-stream of 0s and 1s.

Microprocessor

The bit-stream is put into sections called registers. One register can store a fixed number of bits.

1 0 0 1

Memory

From the registers the 0s and 1s go to the arithmetic logic unit, which uses arithmetic rules to process them.

The result is put into memory or sent through an output to other parts of the system.

Output

Superfast versions

At the other end of the scale the most powerful PCs have several microprocessors working together to do very complicated tasks at high speed, completing jobs that were once only possible using a roomful of separate computers.

Exceedingly high-speed microprocessors are used for handling digital signals and converting them instantly into sounds and pictures, for instance inside a mobile phone (see page 27).

◄ ◄

This photo shows a microprocessor chip embedded in its protective shell, with pins to fit it into a circuit board.

CPU Logic

A microprocessor uses logic to translate a stream of binary data into a set of commands that it can follow. The job is done in the same way as you would do an algebra maths sum.

Logic gates

A microprocessor receives data as a stream of 0s and 1s. These move through lots of interconnected transistors which form 'logic gates'.

There are several different types of logic gate. Each one can process 1s and 0s mathematically to produce an output of 1 or 0 (translating in electrical pulse terms as 'on' or 'off') depending on what was sent to it and what type of gate it is.

For instance, one type of logic gate, called an AND gate, always outputs a 1 if it receives inputs of 1 + 1. If it receives any 0s, it won't produce a 1, only another 0.

Using lots of logic gates the microprocessor can reduce the bit-stream it receives to a shorter, easier-to-handle code that it sends on to instruct the system what to do. A programmer, knowing logic gates and what they do, can create a bit-stream that will make them work the way he or she wants, thus making the whole electronic system perform in a certain way. This is the basis of computer programming.

How they work

This is the symbol used for an AND gate:

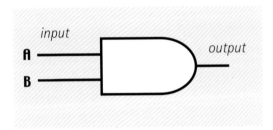

This table shows what happens when an AND gate receives two binary digits.

Input A	Input B	Output
0	0	0
1	0	0
1	1	1

The AND gate will always give these same results, so it's possible to control what the gate outputs and sends on to other parts of the system.

A microprocessor has thousands of logic gates of several different

There are several different types of logic gate and they can be used together in different sequences. Here are three of them.

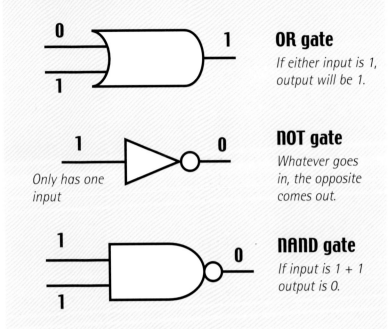

OR gate
If either input is 1, output will be 1.

NOT gate
Whatever goes in, the opposite comes out.

NAND gate
If input is 1 + 1 output is 0.

Only has one input

designs, sometimes working together in groups and able to process lots of data very quickly.

Programming

A programmer doesn't type millions of binary signals into an electronic machine to create a computer program. That would be impossible for a human. Instead we type in groups of letters which represent binary signal patterns. These letters are called 'program language'.

The microprocessor converts the program language into the stream of signals that it then sends through its logic gates to convert into commands.

Very basic programming, for an uncomplicated machine, is called 'Assembler Programming'. More complicated versions are called 'High-Level Programming'.

This diagram shows some common types of logic gates with their inputs and outputs.

On this highly-magnified computer chip transistors are interconnected to make logic gates.

Chip DESIGN

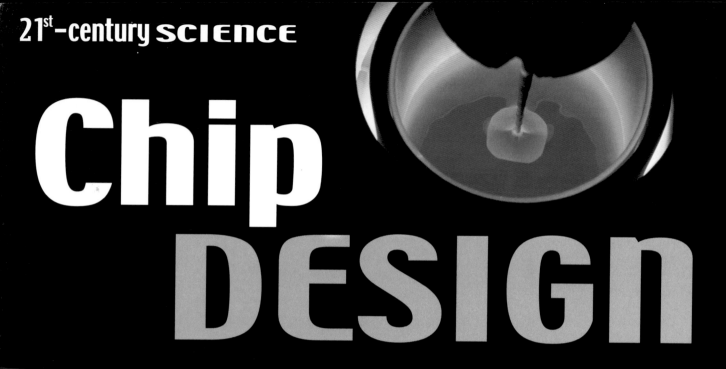

By the 1960s electronics designers realised they could put multiple components together on a single chip. These are called integrated circuits, or ICs for short. The material silicon is used as a basis for the chip because it is a good semiconductor.

Tiny transistors

Transistors are manufactured on a single slice of silicon crystal. The crystal is first grown by putting a seed crystal into molten silicon. This has to be done under extremely clean conditions, in a factory called a 'chip foundry'.

The crystal comes out like a long candle, 10-20 centimetres (4-8 inches) thick. It is then sliced into thin circular wafers that can be divided further into chips. Different chemicals and materials are used to build up transistors and integrated circuits on the chip's surface (see pages 28-29).

Designers began by making relatively simple integrated circuits. Gradually integrated circuits became more and more complicated, leading ultimately to the microprocessor.

Large chips might contain as many as hundreds of millions of transistors. Simpler ones might contain a few thousand on a chip a few millimetres square.

A Pentium D900 microprocessor, designed by Intel and introduced in 2006, has 376 million transistors. The smallest connection on this chip is 65 nanometres wide (a human hair is 80 thousand nanometres wide).

Chip advantages

Chips are reliable and they work quickly because the distances between the tiny pieces on the chip are small. Signals can travel very fast between them. Compared to an old-fashioned circuit board, with big components and bits of wire, they are an incredible advance.

But...

Complex integrated circuits take a lot of time and money to develop. A big chip can take up to five years to design. In addition, the technology to make ever more complex chips work has to be constantly improved, which means new factories have to be built for each new generation of chip.

All this means that the investment in new chips is getting ever higher (In 2003 it was around $5 billion US; it generally doubles every four years.) The only way the chip makers can make money is to sell lots of newly designed chips quickly, before they go out of date.

Inflexible chips

Once a chip has been designed and all the tooling is in place to make it, it would be very time-consuming and expensive to suddenly change the design. However, chip technology is changing so fast that the computing power of an integrated circuit doubles every 18 months! Designing new chips is far too expensive for special applications, so designers have started using 'flexible chips' that can be more cost-effective and adaptable (see page 26).

◄ ◄

The first stage in the manufacture of a silicon chip. A small crystal 'seed' of silicon is rotated in molten polysilicon.

▼

When sliced, the wafers of raw silicon are heated in a furnace to stabilise them.

CHIPS that change

Now it's possible to solve some of the economic problems of chip design by making them 'configurable', which means that their function can be changed after they have been made.

Configurable chips

Configurable chips contain a large number of logic gates. The designer can alter the connections between them by writing a kind of program. This is different from an ordinary computer program, where a series of instructions are carried out one after the other. Instead it is a kind of map. The map is a pattern for how the various logic gates and elements on the chip are connected together.

The designer decides what the chip should do, then makes the right interconnections on the integrated circuit. The map can be stored in a semi-permanent memory on the chip, which means it can be changed at a later date.

Alternatively, the integrated circuit can be made with all the logic gates fully connected. Then the connections which aren't needed can be destroyed. However, with this kind of chip it's only possible to do this once. It can't be changed later on.

These kind of configurable chips are called 'gate arrays' or 'field programmable logic'.

ASICs

A different approach is a kind of halfway house between a configurable chip and an integrated circuit of fixed design, called an Application Specific Integrated Circuit, or ASIC for short.

An ASIC is made from standard pre-designed elements that can be slotted together, rather like building flat-pack furniture or Lego. ASIC designers have a library of logic gates and lots of other components to choose from.

The various elements are put together and once the designer is happy that they will do the right job, the chip can be manufactured.

ASICs aren't as cheap as configurable chips. The design cost for one would probably start at around $150,000 US. But that's still much less than designing an integrated circuit from scratch.

Virtual chips

A few companies have abandoned the cost and risk of manufacturing chips, and have concentrated on designing very clever and powerful processors, then licensing their designs to other companies who pay for the right to make and use them.

Once such is the British company ARM, which designs the specialised processors used in most of the mobile phones in the world.

◄ ▲

People in remote areas can now communicate easily with others thanks to the configurable chip technology in mobile and satellite telephones.

Making a chip

Chips have got smaller and smaller, while increasing in power and performance. Making them is a complicated process. Computers are used to design and manufacture them in a chip foundry.

Preparing the wafer

As we saw earlier, the first stage of chip manufacture is making a salami-shape of silicon crystal (see page 24). It is then cut into thin slices using a diamond-edged saw or very thin wires. Each wafer must be polished and ground so its surface is flat and clean, ready to be covered with lots of identical integrated circuits and then cut up into separate chips.

Masking and etching

A chip designer uses computer-aided design (CAD) technology to work out the circuitry needed on a chip. From this design a number of stencils called photo masks are made, showing the circuitry pattern.

To start the circuit-building process

a layer of impermeable silicon dioxide is grown on the wafer surface, like rust grows on metal. It is then coated with photoresist, which becomes soluble if exposed to ultra-violet light.

The wafer is exposed to UV light shining through a photo mask stencil showing the first layer of the circuit pattern. The exposed parts of the photoresist layer on the wafer are dissolved, leaving the pattern on the silicon dioxide. This in turn is etched away by chemicals, leaving ridges of silicon dioxide on the wafer surface.

Diffusion

Once the pattern has been made on the wafer it is put in a furnace and heated to a high temperature. The exposed areas of the silicon wafer are bombarded with chemical impurities called ions. When they are implanted in the wafer they alter the way the exposed silicon conducts electricity, making it a semiconductor (see page 12).

The wafer is then ready for the next circuit layer to be built on top of the old one. It may go through many repetitions of the masking, etching and diffusion processes before the circuitry is completed.

Another masking and etching stage leaves strips of metal that make electrical connections between the different layers.

Roughly twenty layers are connected together to form a typical 3-D integrated circuit. The exact number depends on the design.

Testing and packaging

The circuits on a wafer are tested with tiny probes to make sure they work. Then the wafer is sliced up into individual chips and very fine gold wire is fitted between each chip and its external pins so it can later be connected up to other parts of a computer system. The chip itself is put into a resin or ceramic box to protect it (see page 20).

◄◄

A salami-shaped piece of silicon, ready to be cut into slices and made into chips.

▼

Chip manufacture takes place in ultra-clean conditions, and technicians must wear protective clothing.

Circuit BOARDS

On their own, chips aren't much use. A complex device such as a computer needs lots of chips interconnected together, performing different functions. They are fixed together onto a printed circuit board, called a PCB.

PCBs

The base of a PCB is an insulating material made of resin and synthetic fibres. A lattice of copper tracks across its surface provides connections between the components fixed to the board. Connecting wires are soldered onto the copper tracks through holes drilled in the board.

PCB design

In complex devices, the design of the PCB is critical to performance. As with chip design, PCB designers use CAD programs to draw up PCBs and then to simulate their behaviour to make sure they work. For instance, a CAD system can check a PCB design to make sure that tracks don't cross each other or that connections are not too long to work properly. The CAD model is gradually modified until it all works properly in simulation.

PCB manufacture

To create the copper tracks on a PCB the base board is covered with a thin film of metal. As with chip manufacture a layer of photoresist gets added and a photo mask of the design is laid on top. Passing the board under UV light exposes the copper that isn't needed for the circuitry. The board is then dipped in acid to eat away the unwanted copper, leaving the usable copper tracks behind underneath the protective photoresist, which is then washed away. The process might be repeated several times to build up a multi-layered sandwich of interconnecting wires.

Once the base board has been finished, it is ready to have the components mounted on to it. Robot machines pick up the tiny component pieces using air pressure, then set them precisely on the PCB, before they are soldered into place.

PC motherboards

Inside every PC there is a complex printed circuit board called the motherboard. As well as providing the physical links between the components at the heart of the computer, it also controls the speed and flow of data sent to other parts of the computer, such as the keyboard and the screen.

However powerful the microprocessor at the heart of a computer, its performance depends on the effective design of its motherboard.

A motherboard showing the various components in place.

◄ ◄

This highly magnified view of the surface of a printed circuit board (PCB) shows the pattern of metal conductors on a base of insulating material.

Electronic SOUND

CD players are a good example of an electronic piece of equipment used in many homes. Here's how they work, step-by-step.

Recording the sound

A device called an analogue-to-digital converter (ADC) is used in the recording process. The ADC measures ('samples') a sound wave and converts the measurements into binary code to be stored on a compact disc (CD). On a typical CD the sampling rate used for recording the original sound is about 44,000 measurements a second.

Once a sound has been converted into a precise store of binary data it can be played again and again, exactly the same, without ever changing.

The CD

The CD stores information in a way that can be read optically. It is made from a clear hard plastic which carries within it a very thin spiral track of tiny bumps which represent the sampling information in digital code.

On top of the track there is a thin film of reflective aluminium and then a sealing layer of acrylic. However, the CD player reads the disk from underneath, through the clear undersurface.

A CD track has to store a huge amount of information. If it was laid straight a standard track would be about five kilometres (two miles) long.

Reading the CD

In a CD player a drive motor spins the disk while a laser directs a beam of light at the track. As it moves over the bumps and hollows in the track, the beam is deflected into or away from an optical pick-up and this is registered as either a 1 or a 0.

Once the CD information has been read it is sent to a DAC, a digital-to-analogue converter, which recreates the analogue wave signal from the digital code. The signal is amplified and passed on to a speaker, where a diaphragm vibrates, precisely matching the electrical analogue signal and creating the sound you can hear.

There are other electronic components in a CD player, for instance to control the spinning of the disk and to store the operating data.

On a CD, scratches don't matter if they are small. Unless the loss of data is really big, the CD player can work out what has been lost and compensate for it by unscrambling 'error correcting codes' embedded in the track.

MP3 players

An MP3 player also plays music from a digital store of information. Unlike a CD, however, the music is all stored in semiconductor memory, in the form of small memory cards.

MP3s don't require all the electronic complexities of spinning disks and laser beams, but they store less information than a disk so the sound quality is not quite so good.

◀ ◀

A magnified view of the surface of a CD, showing the tracks.

▼

This even more magnified view of a CD's surface shows the bumps and hollows upon it.

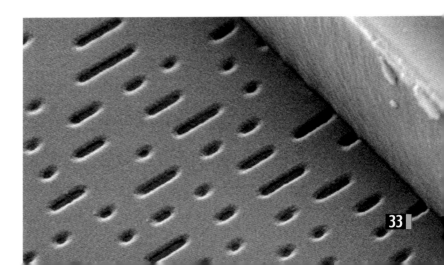

Displays

We see electronics at work when we look at visual displays of information, either on TV or on a computer screen.

CRTs

Cathode-ray tubes (CRTs) are used in old-style TVs and computer screens. They work by heating a wire in a vacuum tube, to emit electrons, which are focused into a beam. The end of the vacuum tube (the screen) is coated with phosphorus which glows in the spot where the beam hits it. The beam moves to draw a line on the screen.

A TV or PC picture is made by drawing lines across a screen very quickly, each one below the next until the picture is filled up. Then the process begins again from the top. A TV picture is made up of hundreds of lines and is renewed around 20 times a second. In a PC there are more lines and quicker picture renewal.

▶ ▶

Modern flat screens rely on tiny fluorescent lights to produce an image.

For a colour display three electron beams are used. Between them they create a picture made up of thousands of coloured dots, called pixels, in red, blue or green. The incoming signal to a TV instructs the CRT when to move the electron beams to make lines, when to start a new picture, how intense the beams should be and how they should be mixed together to build up the colour in the picture.

Ordinary TVs work with analogue signals. Digital TVs use digital signals that can send more precise information. They can have a greater number of pixels on a wider screen.

Flat screens

Plasma and LCD TVs are flat and thin because they don't need CRTs. Plasma screens are made of tiny fluorescent lights filled with gas. When an electric current passes through the gas particles it agitates them so they collide, producing light energy. The lights then glow red, green or blue to make up a picture.

LCDs

Many devices – mobile phones, laptops and now also TVs – use liquid crystal displays (LCDs). In its normal state an LC material allows light to pass through it. If current is passed through the LC material its molecules alter and it blocks out light. A colour picture can be built up on an LCD by passing the light through different filters.

TFTs

Thin-film transistors (TFTs) can now produce computer screens as thin as paper, which can even be rolled up. An array of tiny transistors are connected to millions of minute capsules of charge-sensitive black or white pigment (called electronic ink). A negative charge makes the white particles move to the surface. A positive charge brings black to the top to create black text, making it ideal for e-books and e-newspapers.

Sending the signals

One of the most widely used and world-changing benefits of electronics has been the movement of data over great distances, making it easy to communicate with people all around the world.

Signals via wire

Telephone calls, text, pictures and Internet messages all need to be converted into analogue or digital signals in order to be sent. Then they need to be converted back at their destination, so they can be heard, read or seen.

The simplest way to send a signal is via an electric current through a wire. Ordinary domestic telephone systems work this way. Copper wires connect phones to local exchanges which then connect a circuit to another phone.

When they travel over long distances, these signals become weaker and need to be boosted along the way.

Fibre optics

A more efficient way to send signals is by fibre-optic cable, a very thin strand of pure glass that guides light from one end to the other. Digital signals are converted into pulses of light that are transmitted along the optical fibre.

Fibre-optic cable is able to carry many more signals than ordinary wire. Most importantly, the signals don't weaken as they go along the cable.

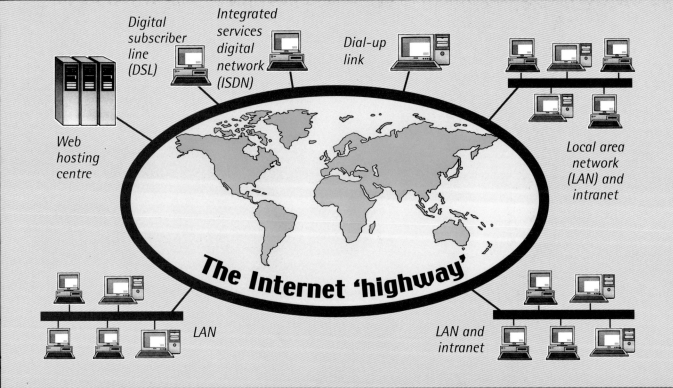

Digital subscriber line (DSL)

Integrated services digital network (ISDN)

Dial-up link

Web hosting centre

Local area network (LAN) and intranet

The Internet 'highway'

LAN

LAN and intranet

Radio signals

Signals can travel through space in the form of radio waves. The waves can be made to carry a specific signal whether by altering their frequency (FM, frequency modulation) or the height of the waves (AM, amplitude modulation). The waves are transmitted and received by aerials.

A mobile phone converts the frequency of a voice sound into a string of binary digits, and does it very quickly so there is no discernible delay in the conversation. The digits are converted into radio wave signals, transmitted and then decoded by the receiving mobile phone.

Increasingly mobile phones can communicate with other types of digital-signal equipment, such as PCs.

Computer networks

The Internet connects PCs with web servers, powerful computers that store web pages and e-mails. It does so via a worldwide network of routers, high-speed digital devices which send information around the world via high-capacity communications circuits. The routers read the electronic addresses on 'packets' of data and send them on to the right computer.

A modem is needed to convert a computer's digital data into a signal that can be carried on a telephone line. A broadband DSL (Digital Subscriber Line) connection gives you a direct connection to the Internet, without having to dial up each time you want to use it.

▲

A diagram showing how the various components of the Internet link together

◄ ◄

Strands from a fibre-optic cable, showing how each strand carries light.

Flying electronics

Electronics is used extensively in civil and military aircraft. Here are some examples of the way developments are revolutionizing air travel and military operations.

▲

In a jet fighter, information from the cockpit's electronic displays is projected onto a transparent screen in front of the pilot.

Fly-by-wire

Modern aircraft have advanced flight control systems which can electronically fly the plane. Input is provided either by the pilot through a small joystick, or from pre-set flight instructions. An onboard computer processes the information and adjusts the plane's controls. It receives constant feedback from sensors all over the plane and can send instructions to control surfaces such as the rudder and ailerons to change course or height.

Many of today's jet fighters and bombers have an in-built instability caused by their unusual design shapes. They need constant corrections to their control surfaces to keep them in the air, using miniaturised digital computers that do hundreds of thousands of calculations a second.

Meanwhile, the many cockpit displays can be projected on to a transparent screen in front of the pilot's eyes or on a HUD (head-up display) helmet. Increasingly these controls are voice-activated, as are weapons systems. On modern helmets a pilot can direct weapons simply by moving his head.

UAVs

Many planes are now designed with no need for a pilot at all, particularly for dangerous military operations. Unmanned Aerial Vehicles (UAVs) are in extensive use for gathering intelligence, and increasingly for attack as well.

Air traffic control

Sophisticated computer systems are used to manage the movement of planes in the sky. Central to this are radar systems. Rapid pulses of radio waves are transmitted through the air, rebounding off the hard surface of a plane.

By measuring the length of time the radio waves take to come back, and the frequency of the waves when they return, the air traffic control system can pinpoint the position and speed of the plane it is tracking, ensuring it is flying at the right height and speed to avoid collisions with other aircraft.

ECM

Military aircraft risk being shot down if enemy radar locates them and fires missiles. In order to confuse the enemy radar pilots use electronic counter measures (ECM), including signal jamming.

If an aeroplane senses that radio waves are being directed at it, the pilot can send back a wall of electronic noise signals to confuse the radar equipment hunting it. The enemy radar sources themselves risk being attacked by missiles that lock on to radar signals.

The electronics that control the onboard weaponry are called the fire-control system.

Sophisticated electronic systems are vital in the cockpit of the new Eurofighter aircraft, shown here.

The **future** of **electronics**

Scientists and engineers are constantly working on new ways to use electronics. It is a very imaginative branch of science, with scope for lots of new ideas. In the near future the emphasis will continue to be on shrinking size and increasing computing power.

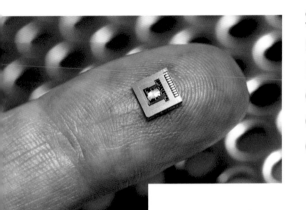

▲

The increasing emphasis on miniaturisation means that electronic components are getting smaller and smaller.

Atomic chips

Already the smallest element on a chip is about 60 nanometres in width (one nanometer is one millionth of a millimetre, 80,000 times thinner than a human hair). Technology is being developed to reduce that to about 30 nanometers. That will mean lots more circuitry on chips until, eventually, tiny devices will be able to store incredibly large amounts of data, creating extremely powerful microscopic computers.

The size limit will only be reached when we make chips with components the size of atoms. At this size the transistor will switch only one or two electrons, and the electrons begin to change the way they behave. For example, electrons can jump through tiny atom-sized walls and interact with light in strange and interesting ways. These are called quantum effects. They open up very exciting new prospects for engineers, and could start a whole new electronic and computing revolution, as big as the one we have seen over the past 50 years.

Organic semiconductors

We now know that some organic materials – such as carbon and some plastics – can be used as semiconductors. Although they are not as fast as silicon chips, they can be used more flexibly. For instance, they can be put into fabric, so it's possible that soon your shirt could monitor your heartbeat, and perhaps even show it beating on a t-shirt display panel!

Organic semiconductors can already be mixed into printing ink to computerise clothing patterns, wallpapers, paper and plastic. This technology is likely to get cheaper and more widespread.

Medical progress

'Lab-on-a-chip' technology is now being developed, which means that a chip inserted into a human body or worn on a belt can download information on vital organs, saving the need for expensive time-consuming tests. Microrobotic equipment will allow surgeons to operate at ever-more microscopic levels, while electronics will improve the performance of artificial limbs.

Already scientists have developed a 'bionic eye', that restores partial vision to blind people. A tiny video camera mounted in glasses transmits pictures of the view to an electronic chip attached to the eye retina. The chip does the work that damaged parts of the eye would normally do, creating an image for the brain to use.

A world of robots

Science-fiction writers have long predicted free-thinking robots that act like humans. The development of complex 'Artificial Intelligence' software programs is bringing the idea a little closer. Machines with artificial intelligence analyse their data banks in order to mimic the human brain's capacity to make decisions.

▼

'Cog', a robot developed as part of artificial intelligence (AI) research, can use its visual system to guide hand movement.

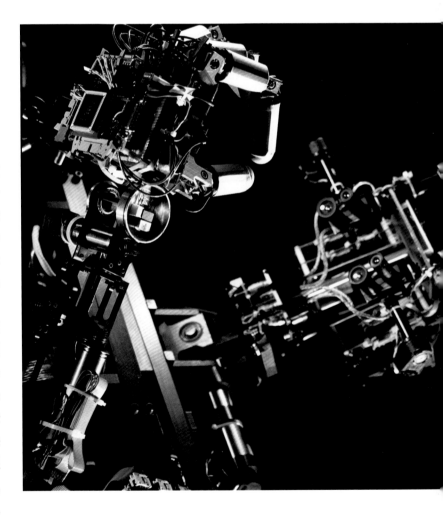

GLOSSARY

amplification
Making a small electrical signal bigger.

analogue signal
An electric current that flows along in an uninterrupted line of waves.

arithmetic logic unit
The part of a microprocessor that processes a bit-stream of binary numbers using arithmetic logic.

binary code
A series of 1s and 0s that represent pulses of energy. Electronic data (information) is sent this way.

bit-stream
A line of binary digits (numbers).

bus
Bundle of wire that carries signals between two different parts of an electronic system.

Cathode-ray tube (CRT)
A glass vacuum tube with a coated screen used to create pictures.

Computer-aided design (CAD)
A technology that is used to design circuitry and simulate how it works on computer before it is actually built.

capacitor
A circuit component (part) that can store electrical charge and discharge it quickly.

Central processing unit (CPU)
The part of a microprocessor that makes the whole system work.

chip
A tiny slice of silicon carrying microscopic circuit components linked by pathways to conduct electric current.

circuit
A pathway along which electric current can flow.

component
A part of an electrical circuit.

digital signal
An electric current measured and converted into a stream of on/off pulses.

diode
A semiconductor circuit component that only lets current pass one way.

electrons
Microscopic particles found inside atoms. They carry an electrical charge.

flip-flop

Two transistors connected together so they control each other. When one switches on the other switches off.

integrated circuit (IC)

A complex circuit with lots of components and pathways. A chip is an IC.

Light-emitting diode (LED)

A circuit component that converts electric power into light.

logic gate

Interconnecting transistors that use maths logic to process binary numbers.

magnetic memory

Method of storing a binary bit-stream of data by polarising magnetic particles to either north or south. The particles are stored in rings on a disk coated with magnetic material.

memory

Part of an electronic system that can store series of binary numbers.

microprocessor

A chip that processes and sends data in an electronic system.

optical memory

Method of storing a binary bit-stream of data by reflecting a laser beam from a surface, for example a CD.

Printed circuit board (PCB)

A baseboard on which electronic components are fixed and connected together.

program

A set of binary instructions put into an electronic system to make it perform a set of functions.

Random-access memory (RAM)

A store that loses data if the power is switched off.

Read-only memory (ROM)

A store of data that cannot be changed, and does not disappear if the power is switched off.

semiconductor

A material which can be made to conduct electricity if its electrons are given extra energy.

transistor

A device made of semiconducting material which can make a small electrical signal bigger, and can switch on and off quickly.

INDEX

These are the lists of contents for each title in *21st-Century Science:*

Energy
Our need for energy • Sources of energy • Electricity supply • Fossil fuels • Nuclear energy • Wind energy • Geothermal energy • Solar energy • Hydropower • Energy from the oceans • Biomass energy • Hydrogen and fuel cells • Energy efficiency • Energy for the future

Medicine
The living machine • Breakdowns in the body • The body under attack • Fighting back • Battling bacteria • Coping with cancer • Complementary medicine • Tools of the trade • Surgery • The genetic revolution • Life in vitro • Medicine in space

Genetics
All about genetics • Chromosomes • DNA • Genes at work • Life begins • Inheriting genes • When genes go wrong • Changing DNA • Gene-splicing • Plant genetics • Mixing animal DNA • Cloning • How will we use genetics? • Genetic mysteries

Telecoms
The pace of change • Signals, senders and receivers • Wires, fibres and aerials • Multiplexing • Networks • Computer networks • Terrestrial communications • Freedom from wires • Cellular mobiles • Satellite communications • The Internet • Broadcasting • The future

Electronics
The world goes electronic • Circuits and signals • Computer building blocks • Memory • Microprocessors • CPU logic • Chip design • Making a chip • Circuit boards • Electronic sound • Displays • Sending signals • Flying electronics • The future of electronics

New materials
Raw materials • Metals • Polymers and plastics • Fibres and composites • Adhesives and superglues • Ceramics and glass • Clever crystals • Silicon • Fuels for the future • Manipulating molecules and genes • Materials in space • Conservation and recycling